P9-CEA-804

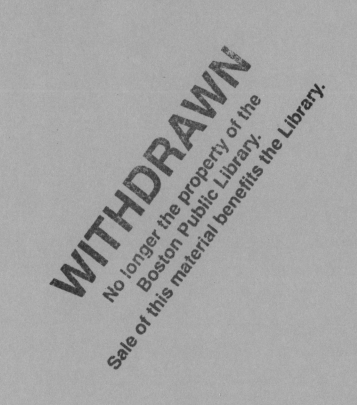

ANN MORRIS

◆◆◆◆◆◆◆◆◆◆◆◆◆◆◆◆◆◆◆◆

PLAY

PHOTOGRAPHS BY

KEN HEYMAN

LOTHROP, LEE & SHEPARD BOOKS • MORROW

NEW YORK

The author wishes to thank Victoria Ivleva for the photographs on pages 20, 24, and 25.
The photographs on the bottom of page 14 and the bottom of page 17 are by Ann Morris.

Published by Lothrop, Lee & Shepard Books
an imprint of Morrow Junior Books
a division of William Morrow and Company, Inc.
1350 Avenue of the Americas, New York, NY 10019
http://www.williammorrow.com

Printed in Hong Kong by South China Printing Company (1988) Ltd.

1 2 3 4 5 6 7 8 9 10

Library of Congress Cataloging-in-Publication Data
Morris, Ann.
Play/by Ann Morris; photographs by Ken Heyman.
p. cm.
Summary: A series of photographs shows that everyone likes to stretch the mind, body, and
imagination in play whether alone or with others including family, friends, and even animals.
ISBN 0-688-14552-3 (trade)—ISBN 0-688-14553-1 (library)
[1. Play—Fiction. 2. Imagination—Fiction.] I. Heyman, Ken, ill. II. Title.
PZ7.M82724Pl 1998 [E]—dc21 97-15728 CIP AC

PLAY

Everyone, everywhere, likes to play.

You can play by yourself

or with others.

Families like to play.

14

So do friends

and animals.

Games and toys are lots of fun.

Stretch your mind

and your body

and your imagination.

Laugh and jump

and swing and spin.

Have a wonderful time!

INDEX

1 NICARAGUA: Some of the best playthings are homemade. This boy has invented his own go-cart. He wheels it to the top of a hill, pushes off, and—*whoosh!*—away he goes.

Title page JAPAN: These little girls are fascinated with the water toys on display in an open-air market in Tokyo. When you wind up the miniature whales, they spout water and swim around the tank.

Half title UNITED STATES: There is rock music coming from the loudspeaker, and these children at a playground in Virginia just can't keep from moving to the beat.

6 BRAZIL: There is no indoor plumbing in some neighborhoods of the city of São Paulo. People get water from a community hose that also serves as a water toy for the local children.

7 EL SALVADOR: Dad uses his bicycle to travel to and from work. But for this brother and sister, riding a bike is just plain fun.

8 THAILAND: A homemade kite and a breeze are all this boy needs to have a good time.

9 UNITED STATES: A game of counting the shells and pebbles just collected along the shore absorbs this young beachcomber.

10 INDONESIA: A teacher on the island of Bali shows his class how to play a singing game.

11 UNITED STATES: Building a sand castle is much more fun when you do it with friends.

13 UNITED STATES: On special holidays this Arizona family celebrates with a piñata. The children take turns trying to hit the papier-mâché bull and release a shower of candy and toys.

13 UNITED STATES: With four kids on one team and two parents on the other, who do you think will win this family tug-of-war?

14 VENEZUELA: These girls are playing a game called pick-up sticks.

14 FRANCE: These best friends share their favorite toys—a doll and a secret locket—at a playground in a Paris park.

15 UNITED STATES: During a game of cops and robbers, the "cops" take a break to discuss the best way to capture the other team.

16 UNITED STATES: Mastering a new trick is play for this baby elephant and her young rider. They are having fun and learning, too.

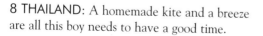
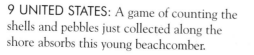
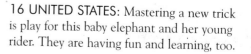

17 ECUADOR: This Ecuadoran boy and his puppy enjoy a quiet moment between games of catch.

18 BRAZIL: This game is something like hopscotch. One of the boys tosses his marker onto the chalk pattern. Where it lands determines what path he must hop along.

18 UNITED STATES: Dodgeball is a good game for recess. There is no set number of players, so everybody can join in the fun.

19 CZECH REPUBLIC: This strategy game was designed for only two players, but these friends like to compete as teams.

20 RUSSIA: This bold pirate captain and his first mate pretend they are sailing in search of treasure and adventure on the high seas.

21 UNITED STATES: This boy is making a model that looks just like his dad's fishing boat. Can you guess what he wants to be when he grows up?

22 UNITED KINGDOM: Ready . . . steady . . . go! These girls look like they are having a wonderful time racing up the climbing ropes in gym class in England.

23 UNITED STATES: There is an open gate into the baseball field, but that's no challenge. It's much more fun to climb over the fence.

24 RUSSIA: A beach is a perfect place to let your imagination soar. Did you ever wonder what it would be like to have wings, like a dragonfly?

25 RUSSIA: In an ice castle you can make believe you are a fiery dragon guarding the drawbridge, or a brave knight, or a beautiful princess, or . . . what would you be?

26 NEPAL: This girl obviously enjoys jumping rope in front of her family's shop in Kathmandu.

26 UNITED STATES: It takes a lot of practice to jump rope double like these girls in Puerto Rico.

27 UNITED STATES: This baby's favorite game is to play patty-cake on the swing with her big sister. The girls are Pueblo Indians from Arizona.

27 UNITED STATES: In almost every culture around the world, children play a game where they hold hands and run in a circle. For these Appalachian children it's ring-around-the-rosy.

28 PERU: When this boy moves the sticks back and forth, the wheel spins. He made this great toy all by himself.

29 GUATEMALA: Pan pipes are one of the oldest instruments in the world. People have been having fun playing them for thousands of years.

Where in the world were these photographs taken?

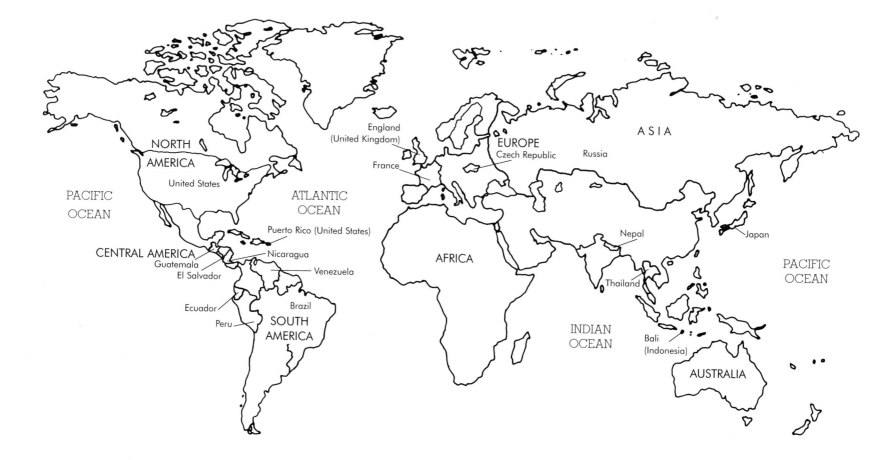